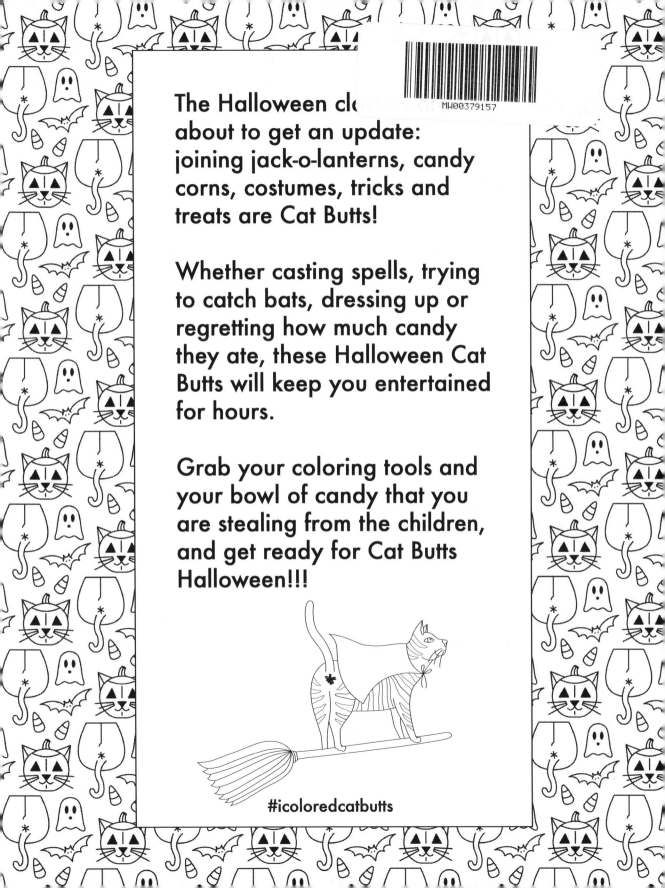

The Halloween cl... about to get an update: joining jack-o-lanterns, candy corns, costumes, tricks and treats are Cat Butts!

Whether casting spells, trying to catch bats, dressing up or regretting how much candy they ate, these Halloween Cat Butts will keep you entertained for hours.

Grab your coloring tools and your bowl of candy that you are stealing from the children, and get ready for Cat Butts Halloween!!!

#icoloredcatbutts

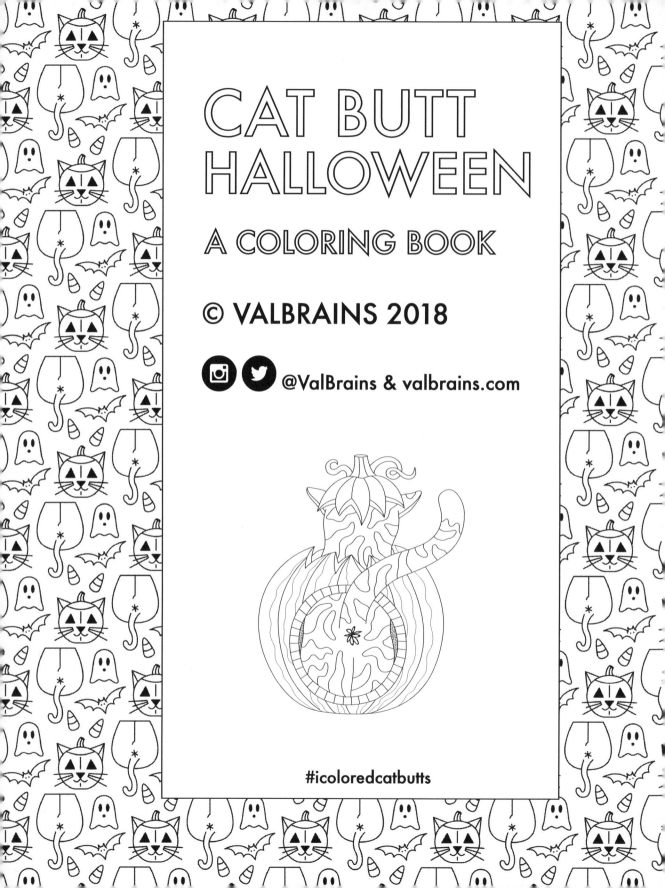

CAT BUTT HALLOWEEN

A COLORING BOOK

© VALBRAINS 2018

@ValBrains & valbrains.com

#icoloredcatbutts

CRACK - O - LANTERN

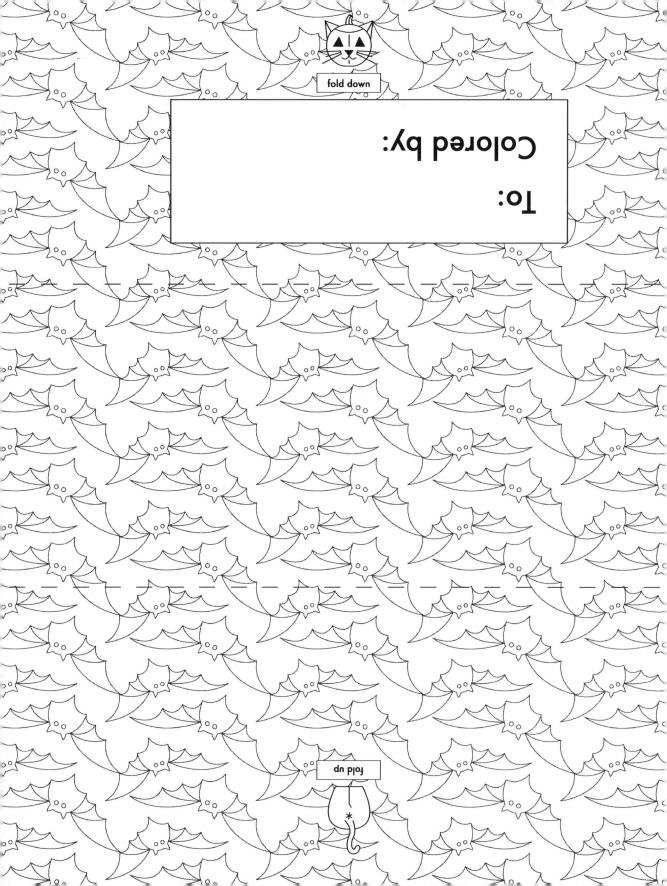

fold down

Colored by:

To:

fold up

I VANT TO SUCK YOUR BAHTT !

fold down

To:

Colored by:

fold up

CANDY COMA

WITCH BUTT ???

fold down

To:

Colored by:

fold up

BATTHOLE

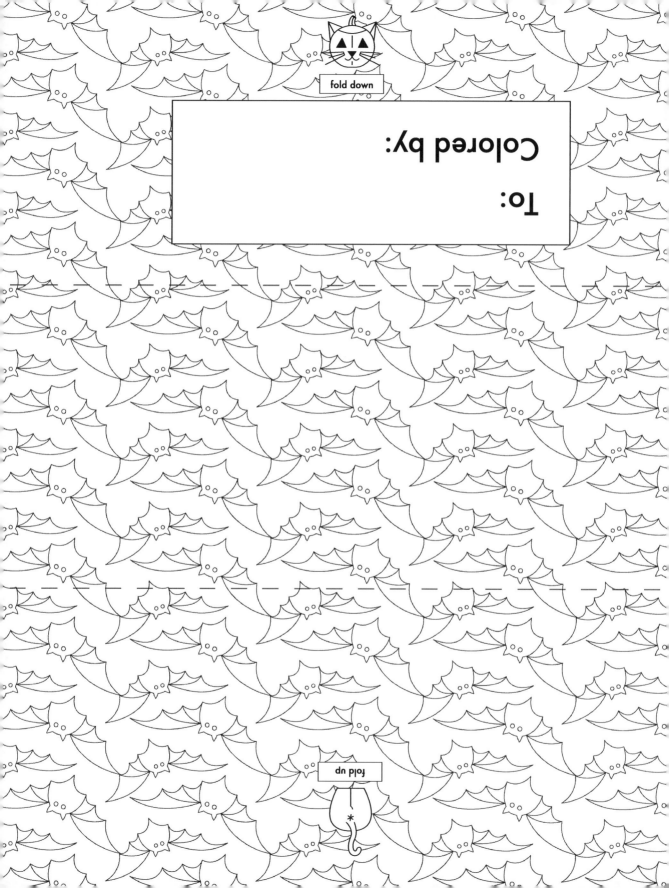

TABLETOP BOTTOM

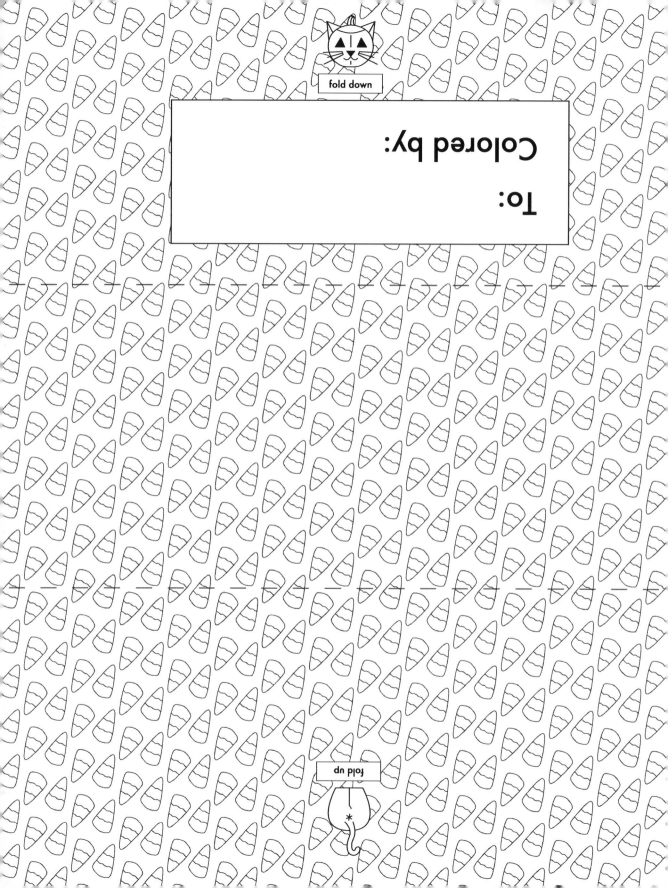

fold down

Colored by:

To:

fold up

SKELETUSH

fold down

Colored by:

To:

fold up

WHAT SPELLS ???

fold down

To:

Colored by:

fold up

CAT BUTT CANDY CORNUCOPIA

fold down

To:

Colored by:

fold up

SCAREDY BUTT

fold down

To:

Colored by:

fold up

BROOM BUTTS

fold down

Colored by:

To:

fold up

FRANKENBUTT

fold down

Colored by:

To:

fold up

PUMPKIN BUTT

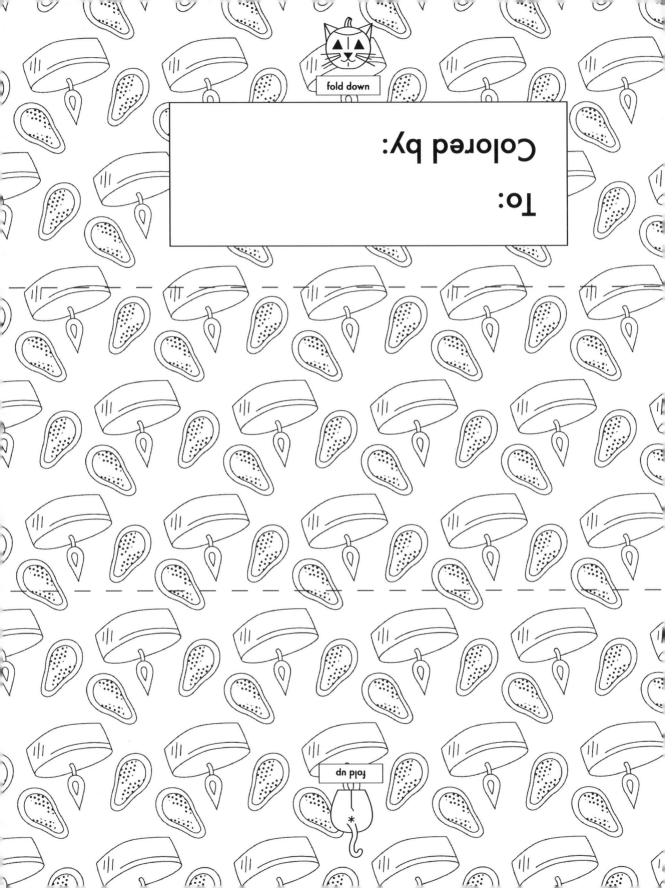

fold down

To:

Colored by:

fold up

POSTERIOR PRINCESS

fold down

Colored by:

To:

fold up

A - CRACK - NOPHOBIA !

fold down

Colored by:

To:

fold up

JUST GOURDGEOUS

fold down

To:

Colored by:

fold up

REST IN PURR

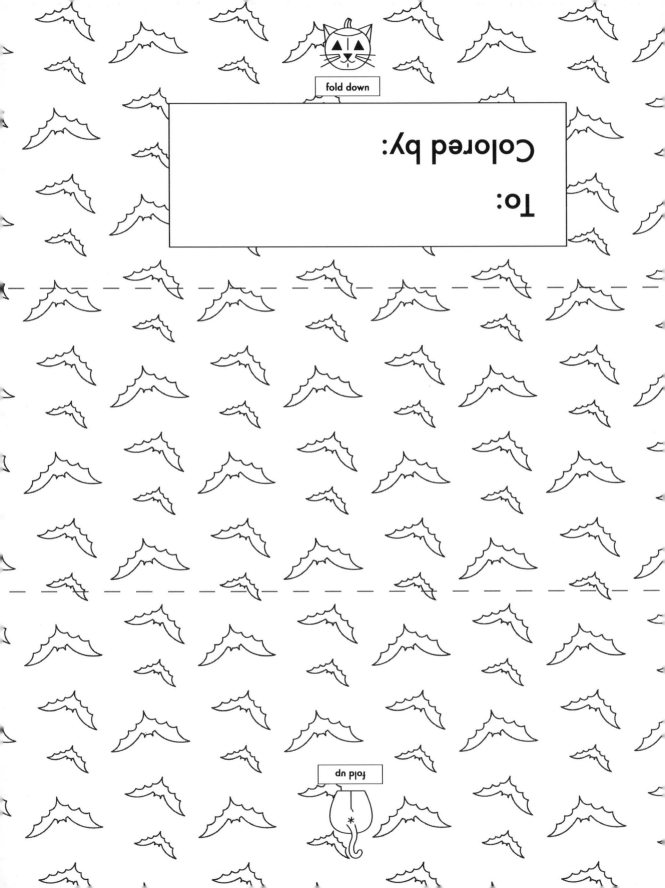

fold down

To:

Colored by:

fold up

CAT BUTT IN DISGUISE

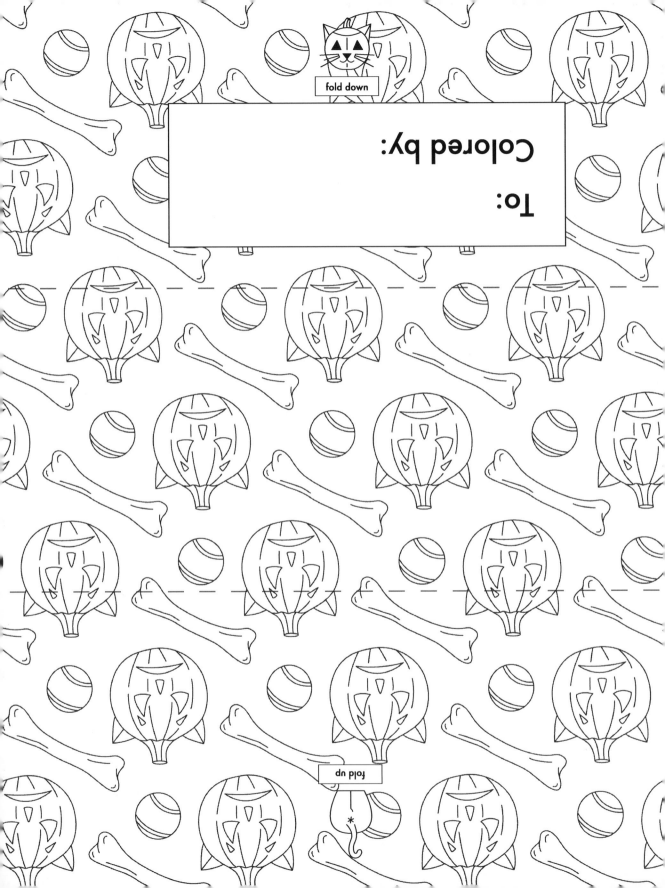

fold down

Colored by:

To:

fold up

HEADLESS CAT BUTT

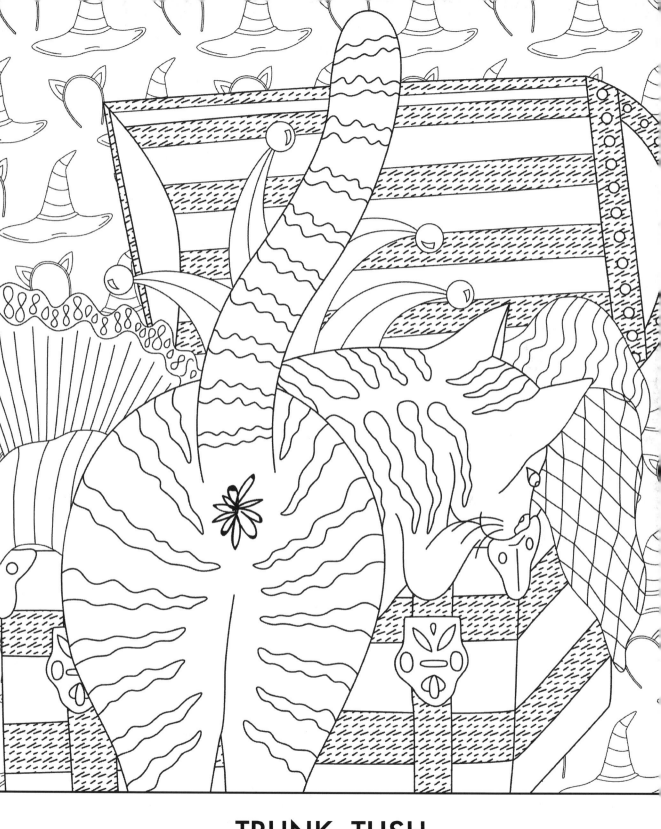

TRUNK TUSH

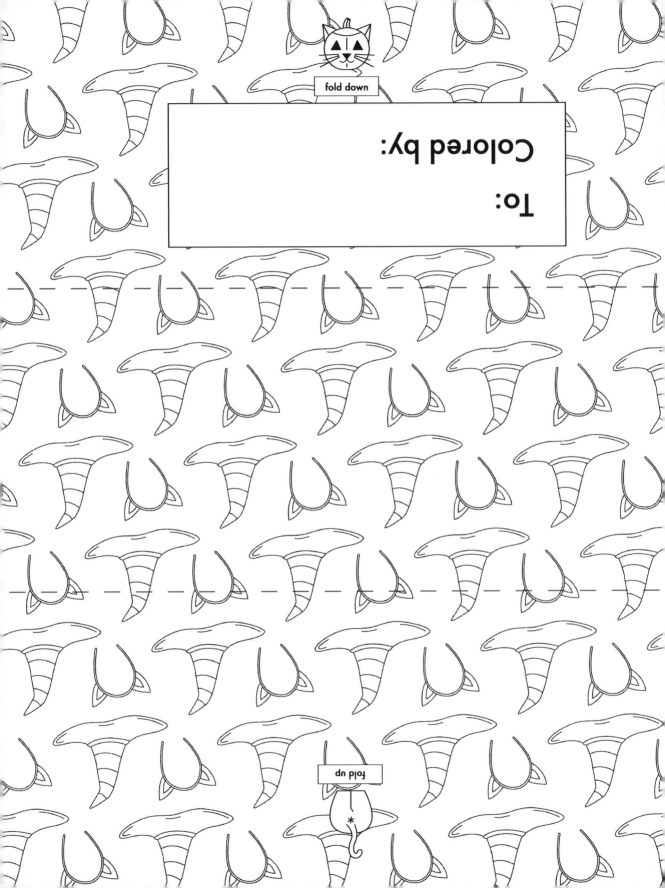

fold down

To:

Colored by:

fold up

A
CAT BUTT HALLOWEEN
HAIKU

All Hallows' Eve has
Some extra hollows this year!
Get it? It's Cat Butts!

#icoloredcatbutts

Made in the USA
San Bernardino, CA
05 September 2019